*A Bedtime Story for Beloved*

# ROWEN

*By Suzanne Marshall*

*Why is this book blue?* The color blue can improve a child's sleep. According to studies, the color blue…

- Promotes tranquility and relaxation
- Reduces anxiety and aggression
- Lowers heart rate and blood pressure

*We wish sweet sleep for Rowen!*

# LiveWellMedia.com

ISBN: 9798853809604

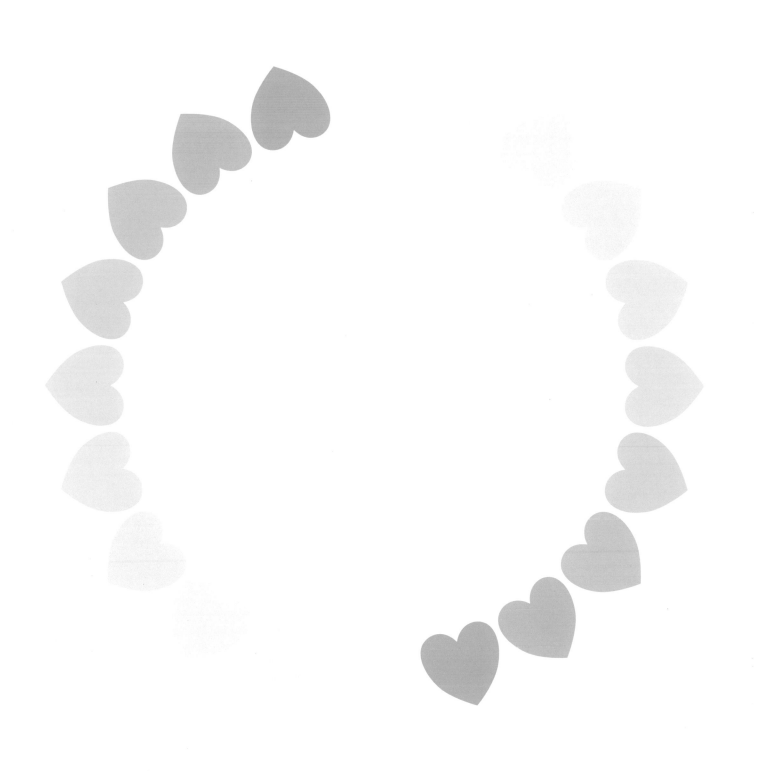

This book is dedicated to

# Rowen

who is loved very much!

Welcome to Bedtime, Rowen! *says the Bear Cub.*
It's time for us to slow our pace.
Let's rest our paws and take a break.

Welcome Bedtime! *says Rowen.*
I am glad it's time for sleep.
I feel great. My day's complete.

*Goodnight Rowen, Sleep Tight.*

Goodnight Rowen, *says the Horse.*
It's time to sigh a giant breath.
It's time to settle, yawn and stretch.

Goodnight, *says Rowen.*
I have done my best today.
I deserve my rest tonight.
When a brand new day begins,
I'll be fresh to start again.

*Goodnight Rowen, Sleep Tight.*

Goodnight Rowen, *says the Lion.*
It's time to enter the land of sleep
where rest is soothing and
dreams are sweet.

Goodnight, *says Rowen.*
Sleep is wonderful. This I know!
Sleep gives me strength to play and grow.
After I rest, I feel refreshed.
After I rest, I feel my best.

*Goodnight Rowen, Sleep Tight.*

Goodnight Rowen, *says the Monkey.*
It's time to nestle in your bed.
So hug a pillow and rest your head.

Goodnight, *says Rowen.*
In my bed I'm safe from storms.
In my bed I'm cozy warm.
In my bed I feel at peace.
In my bed I fall asleep.

*Goodnight Rowen, Sleep Tight.*

Goodnight Rowen, *says the Tiger.*
It's time to gently clear your mind,
relax, release, let go, unwind.

Goodnight, *says Rowen.*
Tonight I blow away my cares
like bubbles floating in the air.
As they float away from me,
I am cheerful, calm and free.

*Goodnight Rowen, Sleep Tight.*

Goodnight Rowen, *says the Leopard.*
Let's put away all noisy thoughts
inside a magic bedtime box.
Tomorrow we can set them free,
like butterflies into the breeze.

Goodnight, *says Rowen.*
Tonight I'll dream of fun
like playing in the sun
and happy times to come.

*Goodnight Rowen, Sleep Tight.*

Goodnight Rowen, *says the Raccoon.*
It's time to shift our attitude
toward thankfulness and gratitude.

Goodnight, *says Rowen.*
I'm thankful for family.
I'm thankful for me.
I'm thankful for smiles,
laughter and glee.

*Goodnight Rowen, Sleep Tight.*

Goodnight Rowen, *says the Leopard Cub.*
Goodnight to us, to me and you,
from head to toes and elbows too!

Goodnight, *says Rowen.*
Goodnight to my feet, even if they're smelly.
Goodnight to my chest and to my belly.
Goodnight to my funny bones and my knees.
Goodnight to every part of me.

*Goodnight Rowen, Sleep Tight.*

Goodnight Rowen, *says the Polar Bear.*
It's time for tenderness and love,
for sweet goodnights
and happy hugs.

Goodnight, *says Rowen.*
I give myself a butterfly hug.
I give myself a lot of love.
I spread my love here and there.
I spread my love everywhere.

*Goodnight Rowen, Sleep Tight.*

Goodnight Rowen, *says the Panda.*
It's time to shine your inner light
throughout your body
soft and bright.

Goodnight, *says Rowen.*
In the quiet of the night,
I fill up my heart with light,
top to bottom, left to right.
I am hopeful, strong and bright.


*Goodnight Rowen, Sleep Tight.*

Goodnight Rowen, *says the Fox.*
Let's breathe together slow and deep.
Let's breathe together for our sleep.

Goodnight, *says Rowen.*
I breathe in peacefully.
I breathe out 1... 2... 3.
I breathe in sleepily.
I breathe out 1... 2... 3.


*Goodnight Rowen, Sleep Tight.*

Goodnight Rowen, *says the Lion Cub.*
Are you ready for your sleep?

Goodnight, *says Rowen.*
I am ready for my doze.
I am ready for my snooze.
I am ready for my ZZZs.
I am ready for my sleep.

*Goodnight Rowen, Sleep Tight.*

Goodnight Rowen, *says the Koala Bear.*
Are you feeling sleepy now?

Goodnight, *says Rowen.*
I am calm and sleepy now,
like I'm floating on a cloud.

*Goodnight Rowen, Sleep Tight.*

Goodnight Rowen, *says the Dog.*
I wish you wonderful sleep tonight.

Goodnight, *says Rowen.*
I will sleep well.
I will sleep great.
I will sleep soundly
until I wake.

*Goodnight Rowen, Sleep Tight.*

Goodnight Rowen, *say the Kitty Cats.*
You are loved to the moon and back.

Goodnight
Rowen
Goodnight

*Pictured above: Suzanne Marshall & Abby Underdog (the inspiration for Live Well Media).*

***About the Author:*** Suzanne Marshall writes to engage and empower children. Her books are full of inspiration and unconditional love. An honors graduate of Smith College, Suzanne has made it her misson to spread love through storytelling. Learn more at **LiveWellMedia.com**.

***Credits:*** All artwork was edited by the author. Heart Cloud (Vlad Ymyr, Pixabay), Sheep (Pisuttardging1, Vecteezy), Bear Cub (Agnieszka Bacal, Shutterstock), Horse (Callipso88, Shutterstock), Lion (Tambako The Jaguar, Flickr), Lion Cub/Cover Photo (Ridzwan09, Shutterstock), Monkey (Elmer L. Geissler, Pixabay), Tiger (Tambako The Jaguar, Flickr), Leopard (Tzvook G), Leopard Cub (Tambako The Jaguar, Flickr), Raccoon (Anna-Lina Eggert, Pixabay), Polar Bear (Gerhard, Pixabay), Panda (SJ Travel Photo and Video, Shutterstock), Fox (Shingo No, Pixabay), Koala (Dominador, Pixabay), Dog (Wirestock, Freepik), Kittens (12222786, Pixabay).

Made in the USA
Thornton, CO
12/07/23 12:33:51

edcca429-0c84-4d9d-88ca-65525e38602bR01